12 QUICK STEPS TO

WRITING WINNING CLASSROOM GRANTS

Bejanae Kareem, Ed.S.

BK International Education Consultancy

www.bkconsultancy.org

BK International Education Consultancy

BK International Education Consultancy (BKIEC) has 20+ years of leadership in the field of education with offices in Atlanta, Georgia and Washington, D.C., USA. Founded in 2012, BK International Education Consultancy's vision is to strengthen educational communities by strengthening educator practices to best serve students. BKIEC is an International Association for Continuing Education and Training accredited provider of continuing education units (CEU).

Services

- Continuing Education & Training (online, hybrid, on ground)
- Curriculum Development Services
- Program Development, Implementation & Management

Online CEU Courses (partial list)

- Grant Writing Master Class
- Google Apps for Educators
- Expanding Classrooms through Virtual Field Trips
- Creating Accessible Learning Environments
- Keys to Effective Parent Engagement

For More Information

Website: www.bkconsultancy.org

Online Courses: www.bkconsultancy.org/courses

Email: info@bkconsultancy.org

Facebook, YouTube, and Twitter handles: @bkconsultancy

Instagram: @bk_consultancy

CONTENTS

INTRODUCTION

The National Center for Education Statistics (2018) reports that over 94% of U.S. public school teachers use personal funds to purchase instructional supplies to support student learning. Given the recent impact of the corona pandemic, teachers' average out-of-pocket costs for classroom expenses exceed $745 annually (Karbowski, 2020). While some schools have essential materials and resources, teachers are often limited in what and how much they can use. However, over $400 billion dollars in grants were awarded in 2019. Grant writing is a much-needed skill for teachers' toolboxes and a great way to access instructional materials, supplies, and tools to expand student learning and alleviate the financial strain imposed on teachers.

12 Quick Steps to Writing Winning Classroom Grants coaches teachers how to leverage their knowledge of creating lesson plans to write a winning grant proposal. The workbook style text features chapter objectives, comprehension checks, grant examples, and templates as a step-by-step guide to producing a classroom grant.

12 Quick Steps to Writing Winning Classroom Grants provides teachers who have little to no grant writing experience with a foundational knowledge of grants, engages them in grant proposal development activities, and dispels common misconceptions about grant writing. Teachers will learn practical tips and strategies to effectively secure funding for their classroom and understand what funders look for when they make charitable investments.

12 Quick Steps to Writing Winning Classroom Grants covers the following objectives:

- Identify the major components of the grant lifecycle and grant application
- Describe the similarities between lesson plans and grant applications
- Identify funding sources
- Draft a basic grant proposal using enclosed grant writing templates to fund a classroom initiative to address students' need

DEDICATION

This book is dedicated to my parents, Constance and Lateef Kareem, for planting the seed of authorship. Thank you for modeling, guiding, and inspiring me to put my thoughts in writing and share them with others. Knowledge is power! I also dedicate the book to my great grandmother, Catherine E. Reed, a former educator who I admired for her resourcefulness and tenacity in finding solutions to everyday issues.

This book is also dedicated to fellow teachers. Many teachers may not be aware they have the foundational skills to win grants. As a former elementary school teacher, I designed this book to leverage your expertise in lesson plan development. So here's to you! I hope you ind this book a quick and easy read that will add a valuable skill to your toolbox and share a way to save your coins.

ACKNOWLEDGMENTS

I would like to acknowledge Magalie Awosika for reminding and challenging me to complete this book. I would also like to acknowledge Dr. Kathleen Champlin, Dr. Adrienne Simmons, Dr. Vera Stenhouse, Ketisha Kinnebrew, Shandra Perry, Shermaine Perry-Knights for your feedback, comments, and edits. I also thank Lexi Smith, Miguel Galindo, Katherine Ahn, Pamela Jennemyr, Kaitlyn Shi, and Tommy Clay for your contributions to this project. Thank you for being my accountability partners. This book would not be as concise without your support and thought partnership.

1

GRANTS 101

This chapter provides an overview of the grant lifecycle. You will learn the components of a **grant application** (proposal) and the different types of grants and grant funders. In addition, you will learn the similarities and differences between **lesson plans** and grant applications. These are the objectives we will cover:

✦ Define grant

✦ Illustrate the major components of the grant lifecycle

✦ Differentiate between lesson plans and grant applications

✦ Illustrate the major components of the grant writing process

GRANTS

Grants are non-repayable funds awarded by a third party (**funder**) to an applicant. Grants are awarded to fund a specific project, have a time limit (usually one, three, or five years), and require some level of compliance and reporting. Grants are often awarded to nonprofit entities or educational institutions. However, there are instances when grants are awarded to businesses (pitch competitions, small business innovation research) and individuals (educator grants, scholarships, fellowships). This book will focus on classroom grants for educators, yet the basics apply across all grant types.

GRANT LIFECYCLE

There are three stakeholders involved in a **grant lifecycle:** 1. the funder; 2. the grant applicant; and 3. the target participant group for the grant. We will focus on you: the grant applicant. Each stakeholder has their own grant lifecycle. See figure 1 for details on the applicant's grant lifecycle.

Figure 1. Lifecycle for Grant Applicant

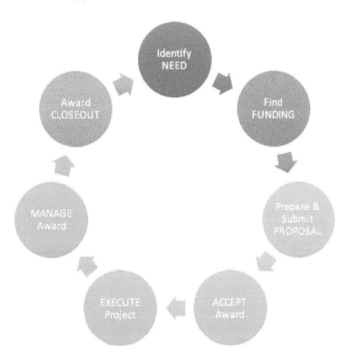

In the applicant's grant lifecycle, the first step is to identify overall needs. Then, select your target group for the grant.

Once you've identified the target group and the needs that you want to address, the next step in the grant lifecycle is to find funding. There are a variety of ways to go about doing this. There are grant email alerts or listservs that you can sign up for (and which may require a nominal fee) which will email you a list at the frequency you designate. You can look up grant opportunities directly from funders by searching their websites. Or you can simply type keywords such as "classroom funding" or "classroom grants" into a search engine to see what is out there related to your needs.

After you find funding, the next phase is to prepare and submit your proposal. The turnaround time for grant proposals varies depending on the number of applications that funders receive. However, the funder will indicate when you can anticipate hearing if you have won or not. Typically, classroom education grants are funded for one year. Larger educational grants may be funded for multiple years, usually up to five years.

If your proposal addresses all of the questions found in the grant application, also known as the **Request for Proposals (RFP)**, you will receive notification you've been awarded the grant along with a point of contact and guidelines for budgeting, purchasing, and reporting. At this point, you accept the grant and execute the project. It's very helpful, during the grant lifecycle, for you to constantly review the original grant application and grant terms to make sure that you are moving forward with the targeted timeline and with activities to manage the award. **Grant terms** are the legal requirements and conditions of a grant set by the funding agency.

Eventually, you will come to the award closeout period in which you wrap up the grant project activities, exhaust your budget without going over, and submit any final reports required by the funding agency or **grantor**.

GRANT APPLICATION VS. LESSON PLAN

So what do grant applications and lesson plans have in common? A lot actually. See figure 2 for similarities between lesson design and grant writing.

Figure 2. Lesson Plan versus Grant Application Venn Diagram

A **Venn Diagram** is used to compare and contrast items or characteristics. The left side lists the exclusive characteristics of a lesson plan and the right side lists a typical classroom grant application's characteristics. The overlapping circles list the characteristics of both. Are

you surprised by how many components of a lesson plan and grant application are similar? Both a lesson plan and grant proposal include an evaluation, a timeline of activities, objectives and goals, and a need. A quality lesson plan should be based on a learning need. Why do learners need to know this content? How do you know they don't know the content? The same is true for a grant application. What is the purpose for the grant project? What need will be addressed?

In contrast, a quality lesson plan includes how the teacher will differentiate instruction to meet varying student needs while a grant application includes a budget to implement project activities. The following chapters will explain each grant application component and how you can leverage your skill in lesson plan development to successfully write grants.

GRANT WRITING PROCESS

In schools, teachers often teach students about the writing process. As a guide through grant writing, figure 3 is a visual aid that outlines the 12 steps for the grant writing process. This is the path we will follow throughout this workbook to unpack the science of grant writing.

Figure 3. 12-Step Grant Writing Process Diagram

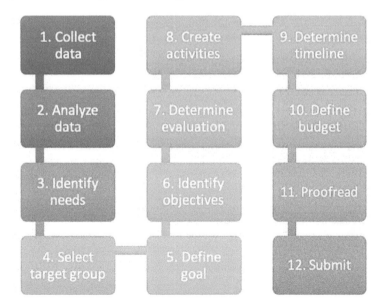

2

DIAGNOSTIC ASSESSMENT

In this chapter, you will learn the similarities between a diagnostic assessment used for instruction and a needs assessment used in grant proposals. We will focus on these chapter objectives:

✦ Define diagnostic assessment and needs assessment

✦ Compare instructional diagnostic assessment and grant needs assessment

✦ Identify the need(s) of the target group

DIAGNOSTIC ASSESSMENT VS. NEEDS ASSESSMENT

A quality lesson plan is based on students' needs. Why do learners need to know this content? How do you know they don't know the content? These needs can be identified by conducting a diagnostic assessment. A **diagnostic assessment** is a pretest used to determine students' individual knowledge levels and skills prior to instruction. It is primarily used to guide instructional planning.[1]

The same is needed for a grant application. The assessment can be accomplished through reviewing the data on hand or conducting a needs assessment in the form of a survey or test.

Once you've identified areas of need, use this information to craft a **statement of need**. The statement of need is your opportunity to make the case for funding. What is the purpose of the grant project? What student problem or student need will be addressed or solved? The funder needs to fully understand the issue at hand before supporting it.

SAMPLE NEED STATEMENTS

In order to craft an effective need statement, the following components must be included:

• Present the need for the project you are proposing

• Use relevant data to establish the significance of the problem

• Directly relate the problem to the proposed solution

---

1   *K-6: What is diagnostic assessment?* (2017, February 27). FTCE Elementary Education K-6 (0-60): Practice and study guide. https://study.com/academy/lesson/what-is-diagnostic-assessment-definition-examples.html

- Specify what the target population needs to learn and why

- Include an illustrated figure or infographic to visually illustrate data/facts[2]

Next are examples of need statements. Which example includes the criteria above? How could you strengthen each statement based on the criteria above? Suggestions are provided in the Appendix "Exhibit 1: Need Statement Examples."

Example 1: The Center on Education Policy (2010) finds that boys lag behind girls in reading achievement. Additionally, our state has launched a literacy campaign to promote third grade reading proficiency because it is a critical issue. Over the years, I have witnessed a gender gap in reading acquisition. It has been a challenge to find creative ways to inspire male students to freely read in my class. Creative and innovative instructional materials are needed to fortify the reading skills of rising male third graders. Through this literacy initiative, second grade male students will be provided with engaging texts to improve academic achievement and perception of reading.[3]

Example 2: According to the National Center for Education Statistics (2009), the proportion of American students obtaining degrees in science, technology, engineering, and mathematics (STEM) is fewer than 27%. These statistics are alarming to us because we have first hand experience of how STEM fields are exciting and have obtained degrees in science. After reading this shocking report, we were inspired to take steps to close the achievement gap and enhance student interest in STEM. During this school year, we will implement the use of robots to improve math and science instruction. Through this robotics initiative, students will be provided with fun, hands-on, critical thinking experiences to deepen their understanding of math, science, and engineering by applying and witnessing them in real-world settings.[4]

Example 3: Data has shown that SEL (social-emotional learning) has had overwhelmingly positive effects on the academic achievement of English learners (ELs) and students who have Emotional and Behavioral Difficulty challenges. ELs and special education students often

---

2   Goldfarb, N., Cole, J. G., & Whitesell, E. E. (2009). *Key strategies for effective educational grant writing*. Thomas Jefferson University. http://jeffline.jefferson.edu/jeffcme/office/presentations

3   Kareem, B. (2011). *Books for boys.* DonorsChoose. www.donorschoose.org/project/books-for-boys/602949

4   Kareem, B. (2011). *Project RoboPandas.* Toshiba America Foundation: Grants Program For K-5 Science & Math Education.

experience high anxiety and low self-confidence. In order to address the social and emotional needs of this demographic while also supporting ways to close the literacy achievement gap between this demographic and the rest of the school, this project has a four-pronged plan:

1. An English to speakers of other languages bilingual classroom library to ensure students have access to literature in their native tongue to help maintain the connection to their culture.

2. 'Book Gift' program at the end of each semester for resource English Language Arts classrooms to promote pleasure reading for struggling readers and at-risk students.

3. Enlarged bilingual section on the County BookMobile.

4. Diverse, inclusive, and bilingual little free libraries.[5]

COMPREHENSION CHECK

Based on the information shared so far, answer the following question. The correct answer is provided in the Appendix.

1. *True or False. Data from a standardized assessment is an appropriate source for identifying target group needs.*

_____

_____

_____

_____

_____

_____

---

5   Simmons, A. (2019). *Diverse, inclusive and bilingual literacy program*. Innovation Awards: Education First and NoVo Foundation. https://selforteachers.org/innovation-awards

NEEDS ASSESSMENT WORKSHEET

Answer the following questions to identify the student needs that will be served by a grant.

What are the needs of your students? Academic? Attendance? Social-Emotional? Behavioral? Lack of skill?

_____

_____

_____

What data (quantitative or qualitative) do you have to prove that these are needs?

_____

_____

_____

If you don't have data, how can you collect it?

_____

_____

_____

Select one need from above to address. What is that need?

_____

_____

_____

_____

Write a need statement that describes your target group's needs, what data was used to identify the needs, and why the needs are an issue.

_____

_____

_____

_____

_____

_____

_____

_____

_____

_____

_____

_____

_____

_____

_____

_____

_____

_____

_____

3

DIFFERENTIATION

Now that you have background knowledge about grants, let's dive into how to identify a target group for a grant. We will cover the following objectives:

✦ Define differentiation, target group, and teaching philosophy

✦ Differentiate between lesson grouping and grant target groups

✦ Draft a personal teaching philosophy

✦ Identify target group

DIFFERENTIATION

In a typical class, students have varied needs. One way teachers address varied instructional needs is through differentiated instruction. Educators define **differentiation** as tailoring instruction to meet individual needs in terms of content, process, products, assessments, the learning environment, or student grouping.[6] While differentiation is not a component of a grant application, we will make a general connection to student grouping for the purposes of grant writing.

STUDENT GROUPS VS. TARGET GROUPS

Teachers tend to group students heterogeneously, homogeneously, or in flexible groups for differentiated instructional activities. Grouping also happens for grants. Grant projects are usually designed around a target group to provide services, interventions, support, etc. A **target group** is a specified group of people who have a specific need.

TARGET GROUP WORKSHEET

Answer the following questions to identify which students you want to serve through a grant.

Based on the need identified in chapter 2, which group of students is in need of support or intervention?

---

6 Tomlinson, C. (August, 2000). *Differentiation of instruction in the elementary grades*. ERIC digest. ERIC Clearinghouse on Elementary and Early Childhood Education. https://files.eric.ed.gov/fulltext/ED443572.pdf

1. _____

2. _____

3. _____

4. _____

5. _____

6. _____

Select one group for whom you have available data. Who will be your target group?

_____

_____

_____

_____

_____

_____

Why?

_____

_____

_____

_____

_____

_____

TEACHING PHILOSOPHY

A **teaching philosophy** is a brief statement about your teaching beliefs and practices.[7] You may recall having to create one in a teacher preparation class. General rules for writing a teaching philosophy are to keep it brief, avoid jargon, use present tense, cite where your philosophy originated, and create a picture of your instructional methods. Including a teaching philosophy in a grant application helps funders take a mental peek into your classroom and gain a sense of who you are as an educator. An alternative to using a teaching philosophy is using your school's mission statement.

SAMPLE TEACHING PHILOSOPHY STATEMENTS

There are a range of styles and lengths that you can use to create a teaching philosophy. Below are examples. As you read them, identify the author's teaching values.

Example 1: My philosophy of education is that all children are unique and must have a stimulating educational environment where they can grow physically, mentally, emotionally, and socially. It is my desire to create this type of atmosphere so students can meet their full potential. I will provide a safe environment where students are invited to share their ideas and take risks. I believe that there are five essential elements that are conducive to learning. (1) The teacher's role is to act as a guide. (2) Students must have access to hands-on activities. (3) Students should be able to have choices and let their curiosity direct their learning. (4) Students need the opportunity to practice skills in a safe environment. (5) Technology must be incorporated into the school day.

Example 2: I believe that a teacher is morally obligated to enter the classroom with only the highest of expectations for each and every student. Thus, the teacher maximizes the positive benefits that naturally come along with any self-fulfilling prophecy. With dedication, perseverance, and hard work, students will rise to the occasion. I aim to bring an open mind, a positive attitude, and high expectations to the classroom each day. I believe that I owe it to

---

7   Cox, J. (2019, September 23). *Four teaching philosophy statement examples.* ThoughtCo. https://www.thoughtco.com/teaching-philosophy-examples-2081517

my students, as well as the community, to bring consistency, diligence, and warmth to my job in the hope that I can ultimately inspire and encourage such traits in the children as well.

TEACHING PHILOSOPHY WORKSHEET

Craft or refine your teaching philosophy below. Include your vision for your whole class and target group pedagogical approach, and what makes you unique as an educator. Remember to be brief.

_____

_____

_____

_____

_____

_____

_____

_____

_____

_____

_____

_____

_____

_____

COMPREHENSION CHECK

Based on the information shared so far, answer the following question. The correct answer is provided in the Appendix.

2. *True or False. English language learners are NOT an example of a target group.*

_____

_____

_____

_____

_____

_____

_____

_____

_____

_____

_____

_____

_____

_____

_____

_____

_____

4

FINDING FUNDING

In chapter 3, you analyzed data to identify a target group and their needs for a potential grant. Let's switch gears to find funding for your classroom. By doing this, you can tailor your grant proposal to match the funder's requirements. This chapter will:

✦ Describe various grant funders

✦ Identify funding for classrooms

✦ Evaluate readiness to pursue a grant

GRANT FUNDERS

Now that you know the definition of a grant, let's explore examples of funders. Below are examples of public and private grant funders that provide educational grants.

List 1. Funders

Government	Foundations/Nonprofits/Charities
National Science Foundation (NSF)	Catholic Charities USA
State Department of Education	Dollar General Literacy Foundation
City Government	United Way

Corporations	Crowdfunding
Google	Adopt-A-Classroom
Target	Donorschoose
Wells Fargo	Classful

The majority of grants comes from the government from tax payer dollars. The federal government has 26 funding agencies. However, these agencies typically do not fund classroom grants. Foundations and charities are types of non-profit organizations. Foundations are funded by a single individual, family, or corporation, and charities acquire funds from donations. Corporations are unique to the grant world. A corporation may offer resources, volunteers, or money to support education initiatives as part of its social responsibility strategy. Additionally, a corporation may establish a foundation by using a small portion of its annual revenue (e.g., 1-5%) to fund various causes, missions, or projects. For example, The Coca-Cola Company is a corporation with a foundation that believes in social responsibility and offers grants. United Way is also a unique non-profit organization; it not only acquires grants from donors, trustees, and other organizations but disperses funds in the form of subgrants. A **subgrant** is a grant created by one organization using funds previously granted to it by a third party.

Crowdfunding is the practice of funding a project or venture by raising many small amounts of money from a large number of people, typically via the internet.[8] Crowdfunded projects are established by donations or investments. Donation-based crowdfunding, similar to grants, typically does not have to be paid back. Investment crowdfunding, as seen on the show Shark Tank, requires equity or return of investment. Educator crowdfunding sites such as Donorschoose, Classful, and Adopt-A-Classroom provide teachers the opportunity to post their classroom needs online to attract public crowdfunders. The teachers do not have to pay the funds back. This is a great place to start practicing your grant writing skills. Please read the terms and conditions of each site for additional details on requirements and stipulations.

FUNDING IDENTIFICATION WORKSHEET

Identify funding to obtain resources to support the target group's needs using the following 5-step process.

I. Websites

Clear the List Foundation | www.clearthelistfoundation.org

Edutopia | www.edutopia.org/free-school-supplies-fundraising-donation

Grants for Teachers | www.grantsforteachers.com

S&S Worldwide | www.ssww.com/grants

The NEA Foundation | www.neafoundation.org

---

8   Calic, G. (2018). Crowdfunding. In *The SAGE encyclopedia of the internet*. SAGE Publications, Inc. https://sk.sagepub.com/reference/the-sage-encyclopedia-of-the-internet-3v/i1840.xml

II. Search Engine

Not finding a grant that is aligned with your target group's needs? Conduct a keyword search in an online search engine. Popular keywords are "classroom funding" or "classroom grants." List potential grants next.

_____

_____

_____

_____

_____

_____

III. Grant Readiness Checklist

Use the Grant Readiness Checklist to help determine whether the funding opportunity is a viable option for your class. If guiding questions 1-8 have checks, the funding opportunity should be considered. Checks in boxes 1-6 indicate that the funding opportunity could be pursued if the missing elements are addressed. Absence of checks in boxes 1-5 indicates that the funding opportunity should not be pursued at this time.[9]

☐ Does your school meet the grant eligibility requirements?

☐ Does the grant align with your teaching philosophy or school's mission?

☐ Does the grant target your class student demographic?

☐ Does the grant provide an opportunity to address your students' needs?

☐ Are your students' needs supported by data?

☐ Has the proposal been discussed with relevant staff members (i.e., school principal, district-level personnel, grade-level colleagues, etc) to weigh pros and cons?

---

9   Stombaugh, H. (2014, December 5). _Decision making matrix. Is that grant proposal worth your time?_ http://justwrite-solutions. com/decision-making-matrix

☐ Is your grant project unique or innovative? Does it stand out from other proposals? If so, how?

☐ What capacity and resources would you need in order to implement the proposed grant?

IV. Grant Scan

Found a viable grant? Next, scan the grant opportunity for the following:[10]

- What is the funding organization?

- What type of funding announcement or post is it?

- When is the grant due (close date)?

- When will applications start being accepted (open date)?

- What type of applicants are eligible?

- What amount of funding is being offered?

- What is the maximum dollar award per applicant?

- Do you have enough time to write the grant proposal?

- What do you need in place before applying for the grant?

- Which potential grants can you apply for?

V. Next Steps

Which grant will you apply for?

_____

_____

_____

_____

_____

10 Aubrey, S. (2014). *Find grant funding now!* Wiley & Sons.

COMPREHENSION CHECK

Based on the information shared so far, answer the following question. The correct answer is provided in the Appendix.

3. *Which type of funder would the Kellogg Foundation be considered: crowdfunding, corporation, or nonprofit?*

_____

_____

_____

_____

_____

_____

_____

_____

_____

_____

_____

_____

_____

_____

_____

_____

5

LESSON OBJECTIVES

Needs assessments and data collection are important for designing instruction and grant projects. In this chapter, we will delve into defining your grant goal and objective. This chapter will:

✦ Compare lesson goals and objectives to grant projects

✦ Define the acronym SMART

✦ Create a goal and SMART objective

LESSON GOALS AND OBJECTIVES

As you know, well-crafted lesson plans include goals and objectives. Grant proposals and projects also have goals and objectives. Goals are broad outcomes of what you want to see in the future. Some examples of goals are:

• Increase literacy rates

• Increase mathematical proficiency

• Increase parent engagement

In contrast, objectives are specific and measurable. Think of objectives as the shifts in students' behavior, skills, or attitudes. Some examples of objectives are:

• To increase the reading comprehension skills of 85% of third graders by 5% on the end-of-course assessment given at the end of the school year

• By December 2022, increase the computational skills of 25% of eighth grade special education students by two percentage points on the quarterly mathematics benchmark test

Goals and objectives are similar in that they describe the expected results of activities and establish the foundation for assessment. Typically, a goal is broad and created first, and it is followed by several aligned and specific objectives. Grant objectives are often trickier to create. Therefore, we will explore the art of SMART objectives.

WHAT IS A SMART OBJECTIVE?

SMART is an acronym for **S**pecific, **M**easurable, **A**ctionable, **R**ealistic, and **T**ime-bound. When creating a grant objective, use the SMART criteria to establish a specific, measurable statement of a desired action. The next section breaks down the acronym further.

SPECIFIC

What do you specifically want your students to achieve? Set an objective that is specific enough to be accomplished. For example: *To increase the reading comprehension skills (skill) of 85% of third graders (target group) by 5% on the end-of-course assessment given at the end of the school year.* The specifics are the target group (third graders) and desired skill (reading comprehension skills).

MEASUREABLE

How will you know when/if your target group has achieved the objective? How will you measure achievement? Establish a criterion (what your students would have to show) for the objective to be achieved. Criteria can measure quantity, quality, time, and/or standard. For example: *To increase the reading comprehension skills of 85% (measure) of third graders by 5% on the end-of-course test (measure) given at the end of the school year.* The end-of-course test will be used to measure student achievement of reading comprehension skills, and at least 85% of the third graders must achieve a 5% increase in reading comprehension. Both criteria are measurements of quantity.

ACTIONABLE

Is your objective something that you and your target group can do? What steps or actions are needed? Create specific actions that will result in students reaching the goal. For example, to increase parent engagement, the following actions can be taken:

- Verify parent contact information (phone, email, and address)

- Create and translate a parent survey to collect data on instructional and family support needs, availability to volunteer, and availability to attend school functions

- Distribute the survey via text, email, and mail

- Analyze data and identify the top 3 needs to implement by the end of the year

- Create a cohort of parent liaisons to collaborate on addressing and implementing targeted needs

- Collect end-of-year feedback on parent engagement efforts

REALISTIC

Are your objectives practical? Are they aligned with your teaching philosophy and/or the school's mission? What support will be needed to accomplish the objectives? Defining a realistic objective is subjective, and you will be the best judge to determine what goals are realistic given the resources and limitations that may exist. For example: *To increase the computational skills of 25% of eighth grade special education students by two percentage points on the state standardized assessment in six months (realistic).* Defining the metric and timeframe is the realistic component of this objective.

TIME-BOUND

When will the objectives be accomplished? Is your timeline realistic for the school year? Allow reasonable time to complete each objective but not so much time that you and your students lose focus. For example: *By December 2022 (time-bound), increase the computational skills of 25% of eighth grade special education students by two percentage points on the quarterly mathematics benchmark test.* "Up to December 2022" is the timeline to accomplish this objective.

By when will this objective be accomplished? *To increase the reading comprehension skills of 85% of third graders by 5% on the end-of-course assessment given at the end of the school year.* If you said "by the end of the school year," that is correct!

COMPREHENSION CHECK

Based on the information shared so far, answer the following question. The correct answer is provided in the Appendix.

4. *True or False. "Increase mathematical proficiency" is a SMART objective.*

_____

_____

_____

_____

_____

SMART OBJECTIVE WORKSHEET

Use the following worksheet to define a goal and at least one objective to address the target group's needs.

1. Write a broad goal below that is an overall intended outcome.

Goal:

_____

_____

_____

2. Write an objective that is a specific measurable action that will achieve the goal.

Objective:

_____

_____

_____

3. Review the criteria below for creating a SMART objective.

Specific Term		Description
SPECIFIC	S	Set an objective that is specific enough to be accomplished.
MEASURABLE	M	Establish criteria (what the student would have to do) for the objective to be achieved.
ACTIONABLE	A	Involve specific actions that will result in reaching the goal and objective.
REALISTIC	R	Given your resources and limitations, is your objective realistic?
TIME-BOUND	T	Identify a reasonable timeline to complete the objective that is aligned with the grant timeline.

4. Revise your objective to make it SMARTer if this is necessary.

My SMART Objective is to _____ (S). I will know

that my target group has reached this objective if _____ (M).

In order to reach it, the target group will do the following _____ (A).

I plan to accomplish the objective by when _____ (RT).

5. Write your SMART objective that aligns with the goal.

SMART Objective:

_____

_____

_____

_____

_____

6

SUMMATIVE ASSESSMENT

Congrats! You've created a needs statement and drafted a SMART objective. This chapter will focus on how to evaluate your grant project and will cover these objectives:

✦ Define summative assessment, backward design, and evaluation plan

✦ Differentiate between a summative assessment and grant evaluation

✦ Create an evaluation plan

SUMMATIVE ASSESSMENT VS. EVALUATION PLAN

Summative assessments are used to evaluate students' attainment of specific outcomes, objectives, or learning goals. Examples of summative assessments are culminating projects, end-of-unit tests, or state standardized assessments. Summative assessments are similar to evaluation plans in the grant world. A grant **evaluation plan** outlines how the grant goal and objective will be measured and assessed. Evaluation requires data collection at the beginning and at the end with a control or comparison group in order to measure whether the changes in outcomes can be attributed to the grant project.[11] Some examples of grant evaluation methods are surveys, focus groups, and interviews.

To develop an evaluation plan, it's key to employ the backward design process. **Backward design** is the practice of looking at the desired results first in order to design curriculum units, performance assessments, and classroom instruction.[12] Starting with the end outcome in mind, rather than starting with an initial lesson activity, better aligns assessments and activities to learning goals to achieve student understanding. Figure 4 identifies the three components of backward design.

---

11 Frankel, N., & Gage A. (2007). *M&E fundamentals: A self-guided minicourse.* MEASURE Evaluation.
12 Wiggins, G., & McTighe, J. (2005). *Understanding by design.* Association for Supervision & Curriculum Development.

Figure 4. Backward Design Process Diagram

Thinking through which goals are desired for the target group, what evidence will demonstrate progress, and what experiences and activities will benefit the target group are significant pieces of a grant proposal.

SAMPLE EVALUATION PLANS

An evaluation plan, as its name implies, is a plan to analyze the impact of specific outcomes, objectives, and/or goals. Here are examples of condensed evaluation plans used in educational grant proposals.

Example 1: To determine if significant impacts have been made, a pre-program assessment will be conducted in the subject area of Geography using benchmark tests. The results of this assessment will be compared to the post-program assessment test and a state-standardized test. Comparing the results of both assessments will help us determine if the project was successful or needs adjustments. Records will be kept of contacts made, frequency of contacts, and duration of contacts. Statistical comparisons of contacts made will also be kept. Surveys will be used to actively monitor participants' perceptions of the program. The results of the post assessment and the statistical contact data will be compiled at the end of the school year. The resulting analysis will be given to instructional leadership to show the impact the program had on student achievement.

Example 2: Project RoboPandas is designed to improve math and science perception and instruction through the implementation of robotics. Evaluation of the effectiveness of the project will consist of several measures. A **rubric** or scoring guide will be created to clarify expectations and assess student work based on specific established criteria. A student survey will be administered to ascertain students' perception of this learning experience. A comparison of second grade project participants and non-project participants will analyze students' achievement level in STEM-related learning.

EVALUATION PLAN WORKSHEET

Use the following to decide which evaluation will best capture the outcomes of your grant project.

1. What data (quantitative or qualitative) will you need to determine whether or not you accomplished your goal and objective?

_____

_____

_____

_____

2. Which method will you use to collect data? You may select more than one if necessary.

- ☐ Survey
- ☐ Focus group
- ☐ Individual interviews
- ☐ Pre/Post assessment
- ☐ Standardized assessment
- ☐ Culminating project
- ☐ Performance assessment

3. Which tool will you use to collect data?

☐ Rubric

☐ Checklist

☐ Observation form

☐ Anecdotal notes

☐ Attendance logs or sign-in sheets

☐ Other_____

COMPREHENSION CHECK

Based on the information shared so far, answer the following question. The correct answer is provided in the Appendix.

5. *Which is an example of an evaluation method?*

a. *Focus group*

b. *Survey*

c. *Interview*

d. *Observation*

e. *All of the above*

7

LESSON ACTIVITIES

So you've identified an evaluation method to analyze the impact of your grant project. Great job! This chapter will focus on the following objectives:

✦   Define project design

✦   Differentiate between lesson activities and project design

✦   Describe activities for grant project design

✦   Create a timeline to complete grant activities

LESSON ACTIVITIES

In order for students to master grade-level content, teachers create instructional activities to engage, expose, and disseminate new knowledge. The purpose of these activities is no different from the purpose of activities found in grant projects. **Project design** refers to the development of activities that strategically align to address the anticipated outcomes, goals, objectives, and needs of the target group. This is also called methodology. In this chapter, you will brainstorm and describe aligned activities and create a timeline to achieve your goal and the objective which will ultimately address your target group's needs.

ACTIVITIES

Given that you are looking for classroom grants, the activities that you put in your grant most often include instructional activities. Remember to identify specific instructional activities, strategies, and/or interventions that will achieve your goal and objective. Be sure the activities are developmentally and culturally appropriate for your target group.

TIMELINE

A project design **timeline** is a chronological plan of how you will implement a grant project from start to finish. It is similar to an instructional scope and sequence where you identify what will be accomplished, the sequential steps to achieve it, and when the instruction will end. The timeline must be realistic and take into account limitations, resources, and support.

SAMPLE ACTIVITIES TIMELINE

Table 1 is an example of an activities timeline for an after-school robotics program.

Table 1. Grant Project Activities Timeline

Date	Methodology/Activity
January	Students will take a pre-program survey. Then, they will be provided with hands-on inquiry activities that will teach them the various pieces contained in the robotics kit and familiarize them with the capabilities and functions of the coding software.
February	While working in small groups, students will design, build, and program robots to complete simple tasks. These tasks will be centered on moving in a specific direction or moving toward moving objects. Students will also evaluate the robots.
March	While working in small groups, students will design, build, and program robots to complete simple tasks. These tasks will be centered on moving in a specific direction or moving toward moving objects. Students will also evaluate the robots.
April	Students will visit a motor manufacturing facility to learn how robots impact our everyday lives. Students will reflect on experiences from Project RoboPandas. They will create, edit, and produce a vodcast highlighting their team's accomplishments, the impact of robotics on our world, and their opinions of Project RoboPandas.
May	Students will create press releases, flyers, and vodcasts to present their robotic programs. The project will be publicized on our school's and district's websites, social media platforms, and newsletters.
June	Students will complete the project survey and the results will be analyzed for program effectiveness.

COMPREHENSION CHECK

Based on the information shared so far, answer the following question. The correct answer is provided in the Appendix.

6. *A _____ is a chronological plan that shows how you will implement a grant project from start to finish.*

    a.   design timeline

    b.   project design timeline

    c.   instructional design timeline

    d.   none of the above

ACTIVITIES TIMELINE WORKSHEET

Use the following worksheet to identify aligned activities to support your goal, SMART objective, and evaluation plan.

1. List specific instructional activities, strategies, and/or interventions that will achieve your goal and objective. Be sure the activities are developmentally and culturally appropriate for your target group.

_____

_____

_____

_____

_____

_____

_____

2. Create a timeline for your overall grant project, including tasks that are needed to implement instructional activities.

Start/End Date	Methodology/Activity

8

LESSON MATERIALS

You are almost ready to submit a classroom grant proposal. This chapter will focus on the objectives below:

✦ Define budget justification

✦ Differentiate between lesson materials and grant budgets

✦ Estimate costs to support grant activities

LESSON MATERIALS VS. BUDGETS

It is common for lesson plans to list materials used for instructional activities. The same goes for grant proposals with the addition of a budget and budget justification. A **budget justification** explains to the grant funder and reviewer what, how, by whom, and why certain items will be purchased. It is a misconception that you can buy whatever you want with grant funds. A grant budget must be reasonable, follow the funding guidelines, and be relevant to executing the grant project.

DEVELOPING A GRANT BUDGET

Budgets are more than cost projections. They are a window into how projects will be implemented and managed.[13] A well-planned budget reflects a carefully thought-out project and provides sufficient cost information to substantiate that the proposed costs are realistic and reasonable for the proposed work.

SAMPLE BUDGETS AND JUSTIFICATIONS

Typical classroom grant budgets include materials/supplies and equipment to support the implementation of grant activities to address the target population's need. However, each

---

13 Goldfarb, N., Cole, J. G., & Whitesell, E. E. (2009). *Key strategies for effective educational grant writing*. Thomas Jefferson University. http://jeffline.jefferson.edu/jeffcme/office/presentations

grant opportunity differs and may allow additional expenses such as travel costs, personnel's salaries, stipends, printing costs, postage fees, and/or consultant fees to name a few. Below are examples of a classroom budget and justification.

Example 1: Books for Boys

Goal: To build a classroom library with engaging graphic novels targeted toward 3rd grade male readers.

Table 2. Books for Boys Budget

Materials	Cost	Quantity	Total
Smurfs #3: The Smurf King	4.67	2	9.34
Bring on the Guest Stars (The Muppet Show Comic Book Series)	7.79	1	7.79
Alex and the Ironic Gentleman CD	23.36	1	23.36
Dodger and Me MP3 CD	19.49	1	19.49
The Incredible Shrinking Kid (Stink Series #1)	12.48	1	12.48
Night of the New Magicians (Magic Tree House Series #35)	11.69	1	11.69
Here Comes the Strikeout: (I Can Read Book Series: Level 2)	3.11	3	9.33
Sammy Sosa	3.11	3	9.33
The Adventures of Super Diaper Baby (Captain Underpants Series)	4.67	2	9.34
Subtotal	$112.15 USD		
Sales Tax + Shipping & Handling	$19.26 USD		
TOTAL	**$131.41 USD**		

Budget Justification: The selection of books is designed to engage boys in reading, but female students will benefit just as much. As a result, students will gain a heightened sensitivity to the powerful and enjoyable impact of literacy! Without these literacy resources, student growth in reading would remain limited.

Example 2: Project RoboPandas

Goal: To strengthen science and mathematics knowledge through the use of robotics.

Table 3. Project RoboPandas Budget

Item/Description	Quantity	Price
Robotics Kit	3	558.00
Video Camcorder	1	65.00
Digital Microphone	1	89.99
Motor Manufacturing Facility Tour	1	0.00
Subtotal	$712.99 USD	
Sales Tax + Shipping & Handling	$31.13 USD	
TOTAL	**$744.12 USD**	

Budget Justification: Project RoboPandas helps students deepen their understanding of science and mathematics concepts by applying and witnessing these concepts in a real-world setting. Small groups of students will design and build robots using the robotics kits. The coding software will be utilized to program the robots and complete various tasks that increase in difficulty. Upon completion of this component of the project, students will visit a motor manufacturing facility to learn firsthand how robots are utilized in building cars. Students will use the video camcorder to digitally document the field trip and each robotics lesson. The footage will be used to share and present a series of vodcasts detailing Project RoboPandas from its initial stages to the final field trip. The digital microphone is a critical tool for recording and editing audio clips for the vodcasts.

COMPREHENSION CHECK

Based on the information shared so far, answer the following question. The correct answer is provided in the Appendix.

7. *True or False. Grant budgets allow unlimited purchasing types and spending.*

_____

_____

_____

BUDGET TEMPLATE

Use the following template to identify costs for items you need to implement your grant project. Remember that the items listed should support the project and address your target group's needs based on evidence from data. Include taxes and shipping and handling for each item.

Budget Item	Item	Quantity	Amount
Materials/Supplies			
1			
2			
3			
Equipment			
1			
2			
Printing Costs			
1			
2			
Postage Fees			
1			
Other			
1			
Total			

BUDGET JUSTIFICATION

Draft a budget justification below. Remember to substantiate the proposed costs as reasonable and necessary.

_____

_____

_____

_____

_____

_____

_____

_____

_____

_____

_____

_____

_____

_____

_____

_____

_____

_____

9

LESSON DRAFT AND SUBMISSION

Now that you understand the similarities between a lesson plan and a grant proposal, let's discuss next steps for drafting your proposal and preparing to submit it. This chapter will focus on these objectives:

+ List common grant proposal sections

+ Differentiate between lesson and grant submission

+ Define submittal

+ Determine next steps after notification of award

GRANT PROPOSAL SECTIONS

Grant proposal sections vary by funder; however, there are similarities among most proposals. Figure 5 lists the typical sections of a classroom grant proposal. As you draft your proposal, be careful to follow the funder's template and complete the sections as directed.

Figure 5. Common Grant Sections

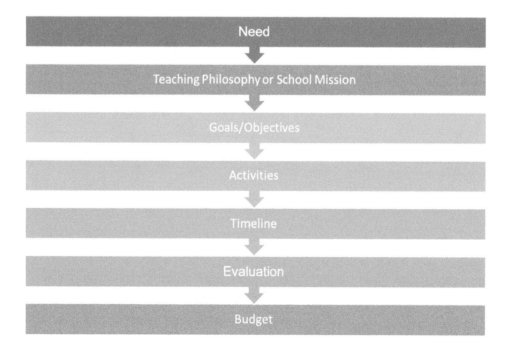

SAMPLE GRANT PROPOSALS

As a teacher, I remember that it was helpful to have a template or sample of the official documents that I needed to submit. Here are two examples of classroom grants created and submitted by teachers like you. As you review them, identify the essential grant components (e.g., need, objectives, timeline etc). How could you strengthen each application with the criteria you've learned throughout this workbook? If you were a funder, would you fund each proposal? Suggestions are provided in the Appendix "Exhibit 2: Sample Grant Proposals."

Example 1: Books for Boys

It has been a challenge to find creative ways to inspire male students to freely read. In an effort to fortify the reading skills of my male students, I will utilize graphic novels to address their literacy apathy and deficiencies.

My school is located in an urban city. The facility is recognized as a Title I public school with over 400 students enrolled in pre-kindergarten to 5th grade. The student population is comprised of 77% African-American, 13% White, 6% Hispanic and 4% Asian students. The Center on Education Policy (2010) finds that boys lag behind girls in reading achievement. Over the years, I have also witnessed a gender gap in reading acquisition. Creative and innovative instructional materials must be used to fortify the reading skills of rising third graders. From this literacy initiative, students will be provided with engaging texts to improve academic achievement and student perceptions of reading.

My students need 30+ graphic novels as a motivator to foster a love of reading! The objective of this literacy project is to motivate and engage boys in literacy learning through the use of graphic novels and books geared toward boys' interests. An initial reading diagnostic assessment will be given to establish baseline data for each student. Students' reading progress will constantly be monitored through grant resources. As a culminating activity, students will create digital stories of their own. Students will be evaluated on the content quality of their stories. A summative assessment will be given to measure students' improvement in reading comprehension and vocabulary acquisition after they use grant resources. As a result, my students will gain a heightened sensitivity to the powerful and enjoyable impact of literacy!

Materials	Cost	Quantity	Total
Smurfs #3: The Smurf King	4.67	2	9.34
Bring on the Guest Stars (The Muppet Show Comic Book Series)	7.79	1	7.79
Alex and the Ironic Gentleman CD	23.36	1	23.36
Dodger and Me MP3 CD	19.49	1	19.49
The Incredible Shrinking Kid (Stink Series #1)	12.48	1	12.48
Night of the New Magicians (Magic Tree House Series #35)	11.69	1	11.69
Here Comes the Strikeout: (I Can Read Book Series: Level 2)	3.11	3	9.33
Sammy Sosa	3.11	3	9.33
The Adventures of Super Diaper Baby (Captain Underpants Series)	4.67	2	9.34
Subtotal	$112.15 USD		
Sales Tax + Shipping & Handling	$19.26 USD		
TOTAL	**$131.41 USD**		

Participation in this literacy project would add an element of excitement and increased engagement for male students and encourage them to complete their literacy tasks. The selection of books is designed to engage boys in reading, but female students will benefit just as much. Without these literacy resources, student growth as readers would remain limited. Thank you for your consideration in supporting and promoting Books for Boys.

Example 2: Project RoboPandas

Project RoboPandas helps students deepen their understanding of math, science, and engineering concepts by applying and witnessing them in a real world setting. Students will design, build, test, and program robots using robotics kits to complete various tasks that increase in difficulty from moving objects to maneuvering along a path with obstacles. Upon completion of this component of the project, students will visit a vehicle manufacturing plant to learn firsthand how robots are utilized in building cars. As the culmination of the project, students will create vodcasts to share their gained knowledge.

According to the National Center for Education Statistics (2009), the proportion of American students obtaining degrees in science, technology, engineering, and mathematics (STEM), is less than 27%. These statistics are alarming to me because I have firsthand experience of how STEM fields are exciting and have obtained a degree in science.

After reading this shocking report, I was inspired to take steps to close the achievement gap and enhance student interest in STEM. During this school-year, I will implement the use of robots to improve math and science instruction. Through this robotics initiative, students will be provided with fun, hands-on, critical thinking experiences to deepen their understanding of math, science, and engineering concepts by applying and witnessing them in a real-world setting. Students will share their gained knowledge by creating and posting STEM vodcasts online. The vodcasts will illustrate Project RoboPandas, and how robots impact our lives, for our school community and a global audience.

Project RoboPandas integrates problem-solving and authentic collaboration to promote high academic achievement. This project is a different approach to teaching math, science, and technology at the elementary level; it will enhance student interest in STEM and teach science in a way that helps children develop inquiry ability, a love of science and math, and the ability to develop critical thinking skills. The project will impact the way students learn because it will allow students to explore their natural curiosity about robots, test their own scientific questions, and integrate their love of technology. I strongly believe if students are provided with proper tools and instruction, they can succeed!

The method of instruction for Project RoboPandas is to divide students into small collaborative groups guided by a teacher-coach (myself) and a local community mentor for one hour twice a week. Mentors from local colleges have agreed to participate in this project.

Teams will design, build, test, and program robots using the robotics kits. The robots will be programmed to complete various tasks that increase in difficulty from moving objects to maneuvering along a path with obstacles. Each group will consist of a team lead, a videographer, an engineer, and a programmer. The team lead will delegate tasks and set goals for the group. The videographer will record the team's efforts using cameras and videos. The engineer will design and build a robot to meet specific criteria and complete various tasks. The programmer will utilize the coding software to achieve assigned missions. Upon completion of this component of the project, students will visit a motor manufacturing facility to learn firsthand how robots are utilized in building cars.

As a culmination to Project RoboPandas, students will take part in writing, editing, and producing a STEM vodcast to present their project online using a video and audio production application. Each collaborative group will create a script, edit, select appropriate music and videos, and record a podcast with fluency and expression. Project RoboPandas is designed to include twenty students in second grade and expand to include additional grade levels each following year. The project implementation timeline is as follows:

January - students will be provided with hands-on inquiry activities that will teach them the various pieces contained in the robotics kit and familiarize them with the capabilities and functions of the coding software.

February - while working in small groups, students will design, build, and program robots to complete simple tasks. These tasks will be centered on moving in a specific direction or moving toward moving objects. Students will also evaluate the robots.

March - while working in small groups, students will design, build, and program robots to complete simple tasks. These tasks will be centered on moving in a specific direction or moving toward moving objects. Students will also evaluate the robots.

April - students will visit a motor manufacturing facility to learn how robots impact our everyday lives. Students will reflect on experiences from Project RoboPandas. They will create, edit, and produce a vodcast highlighting their team's accomplishments, how robots impact our world, and their opinions of Project RoboPandas.

May - our class will also create press releases and flyers for several media outlets and community partners. The project will be publicized on our school's and district's websites (in the form of a webcast), Twitter feeds, Facebook pages, and newsletters. Students will present their robotics programs and vodcasts to the school community. Vodcasts will also be hosted online for the broader global community.

Project RoboPandas is designed to improve math and science perception and instruction through the implementation of robotics. The effectiveness of the project will be evaluated through several measures. A rubric will be created to clarify expectations and assess student work based on specific established criteria. A student survey will be administered to ascertain students' perceptions of this learning experience. A comparison of second grade project participants and non-project participants will analyze students' achievement levels in STEM-related learning.

Item/Description	Quantity	Price
Robotics Kit	3	558.00
Video Camcorder	1	65.00
Digital Microphone	1	89.99
Subtotal	$712.99 USD	
Sales Tax + Shipping & Handling	$31.13 USD	
TOTAL	**$744.12 USD**	

Project RoboPandas helps students deepen their understanding of science and mathematics concepts by applying and witnessing them in a real-world setting. Small groups of students will design and build robots using the robotics kits. The coding software will be utilized to program the robots and complete various tasks that increase in difficulty. Upon completion of this component of the project, students will visit a motor manufacturing facility to learn firsthand how robots are utilized in building cars. Students will use the video camcorder to digitally document the field trip and each robotics lesson. The footage will be used to present and share a series of vodcasts detailing Project RoboPandas from its initial stages to the final field trip. The digital microphone is a critical tool for recording and editing audio clips for the vodcasts.

GRANT REVIEW TIPS

Before submitting your grant proposal, it's helpful to follow these tips. Many are tips for clear writing that you've shared with your students.

- Review ALL proposal instructions and follow them precisely

- Answer each proposal question/section explicitly

- Include visuals when appropriate

- Get the school administrator's approval to submit

- Have a third party proofread your proposal for clarity and grammatical errors

- Don't wait until the last minute!

LESSON SUBMISSION

Part of the lesson plan process is submitting your lesson for review or feedback from a school administrator prior to implementation. Similarly, the grant writing process includes a review phase and submittal. Review your proposal against the grant rubric if one was provided. This will ensure that you are addressing all of the requirements and questions. A **submittal** is another term for a submitted grant proposal. Submit your grant proposal and print out or screenshot the confirmation email to confirm that your grant was submitted.

NEXT STEPS

After the grant deadline, your proposal will be assessed. After the grant review period, you will receive notification if you've been awarded the grant along with a point of contact and guidelines for purchasing and reporting. If you have not received notification, check the funder's website for an award announcement.

If you've been awarded, now what? You will enter into the following stages of the grant lifecycle found in chapter 1: Accept Award, Execute Project, Manage Award, and Award Closeout. We will describe what you can generally expect during each phase.

Figure 6. Lifecycle for Grant Applicant

ACCEPT AWARD

- Wait for receipt of the **Notice of Award** (NOA)

- You will be assigned a point of contact who will answer questions, discuss challenges, and receive reports

- Execute the grant terms

EXECUTE PROJECT

- Comply with the grant terms and conditions

- Complete the activities defined in the grant timeline

MANAGE AWARD

- Adhere to the programmatic and financial reporting procedures

- Conduct an evaluation plan

AWARD CLOSEOUT

- Submit your final financial and programmatic reports

- The point of contact will confirm if all grant work and tasks are completed

- Retain the grant records for at least 5-10 years from the date of the final expenditure report

What if you weren't so lucky this go round with your grant? If you weren't awarded, now what? Don't take it personally. They rejected your proposal – not you! Here are some steps to take.

- Verify whether or not you followed all RFP guidelines

- Contact the funder and request a copy of the reviewer's comments[14]

- Sometimes the funder will post the awarded proposals. Learn from the strengths of the other proposals and apply those best practices

- Revise and resubmit your application for the next funding cycle if this is feasible

- Identify another grant to apply for

---

14 Ransom, J. (2018, January 11). *Ten things you should do if your grant proposal is rejected*. Bloomerang. https://bloomerang.co/blog/10-things-you-should-do-if-your-grant-proposal-is-rejected/

COMPREHENSION CHECK

Based on the information shared so far, answer the following question. The correct answer is provided in the Appendix.

8. *What does the acronym* NOA *mean?*

_____

_____

_____

_____

_____

_____

_____

_____

_____

_____

_____

_____

_____

_____

GRANT APPLICATION TEMPLATE

Use the following template to draft your proposal before submission. This form is best used as a Word or Google document so you can utilize the word count, font size, font style, and spellcheck functions. This will also make it convenient for your proofreader to access the document and make comments and edits.

Question/ Category	Your Answer/Response	**Notes** (include any notes to remember from the grant (e.g., maximum number of words in a section, font size, etc).
Example		
Project Title	*Books for Boys*	*Maximum 10 words*
School Name	*Mountain View*	
First Name	*Iva*	*Please list primary contact from school*
Last Name	*Grant*	
What's your position or job title?	*4th grade English Language Arts teacher*	
Describe your students' need and how you plan to address it.		*Maximum 200 words*
Begin Writing Your Grant Below		
Question/ Category	Your Answer/Response	**Notes** (include any notes to remember from the grant (e.g., maximum number of words in a section, font size, etc).

APPENDIX

INDEX

COMPREHENSION CHECK ANSWERS

1. True

2. False

3. Nonprofit

4. False

5. E. All of the above

6. B. Project design timeline

7. False

8. Notification of Award

EXHIBIT 1. NEED STATEMENT EXAMPLES

Examples	Criteria Addressed			
Criteria	Ex. 1	Ex. 2	Ex. 3	Comments
Need identified	☑	☑	☑	
Data/Evidence	☑	☑	☑	
Solution solves problem	☑	☑	☑	
Target population	☑	☑	☑	Ex 2 could be strengthened by identifying a specific target audience.
Graphics				A graphic would help to illustrate each need statement. Include graphics whenever possible in order to break up text for grant reviewers who are visual learners.

EXHIBIT 2. SAMPLE GRANT PROPOSALS

Proposals	Essential Grant Elements		
Criteria	Ex. 1	Ex. 2	Comments
Need	☑	☑	
Goal	☑	☑	
Objective(s)	☑	☑	An objective was included in Ex. 1; however, it was not SMART. It was not specific and measurable.
Evaluation	☑	☑	
Activities		☑	Ex. 1 generally mentioned activities but gave limited details on how the target group would engage with the graphic novels in order to address literacy apathy and deficiencies.
Timeline		☑	No timeline was provided in Ex. 1.
Budget	☑	☑	

REFERENCES

Aubrey, S. (2014). *Find grant funding now!* Wiley & Sons.

Calic, G. (2018). Crowdfunding. In *The SAGE encyclopedia of the internet.* SAGE Publications, Inc. https://sk.sagepub.com/reference/the-sage-encyclopedia-of-the-internet-3v/i1840.xml

Center on Education Policy. (2010, March). *Are there differences in achievement between boys and girls?* https://files.eric.ed.gov/fulltext/ED509023.pdf

Congressional Research Service. (2019, May 22). *Federal grants to state and local governments: A historical perspective on contemporary issues.* https://fas.org/sgp/crs/misc/R40638.pdf

Cox, J. (2019, September 23). *Four teaching philosophy statement examples.* ThoughtCo. https://www.thoughtco.com/teaching-philosophy-examples-2081517

Doran, G. (1981). *There's a S.M.A.R.T. way to write management's goals and objectives.* Management Review. 70 (11): 35–36.

Frankel, N., & Gage A. (2007). *M&E fundamentals: A self-guided minicourse.* MEASURE Evaluation.

Fundamental grant proposal template: 8 crucial components. (2018, April 17). Snowball fundraising. https://snowballfundraising.com/grant-proposal-template

Goldfarb, N., Cole, J. G., & Whitesell, E. E. (2009). *Key strategies for effective educational grant writing.* Thomas Jefferson University. http://jeffline.jefferson.edu/jeffcme/office/presentations

K-6: What is diagnostic assessment? (2017, February 27). FTCE Elementary Education K-6 (0-60): Practice and study guide. https://study.com/academy/lesson/what-is-diagnostic-assessment-definition-examples.html

REFERENCES

Karbowski, D. (2020, June 15). *Teachers spend $745 a year on supplies: The cost of distance learning.* Adopt A Classroom. https://www.adoptaclassroom.org/2020/06/15/teachers-spend-745-a-year-on-supplies-the-cost-of-distance-learning

Kareem, B. (2011). *Books for boys.* DonorsChoose. https://www.donorschoose.org/project/books-for-boys/602949

Kareem, B. (2011). *Project RoboPandas.* Toshiba America Foundation: Grants Program For K-5 Science & Math Education.

National Center for Education Statistics. (2018, May). *Public school spending on classroom supplies. Data point. NCES 2018-097.* U.S. Department of Education. https://files.eric.ed.gov/fulltext/ED583062.pdf

National Center for Education Statistics. (2009, July). *Students who study science, technology, engineering, and mathematics (STEM) in postsecondary education. Stats in brief: NCES 2009-161.* U.S. Department of Education. https://nces.ed.gov/pubs2009/2009161.pdf

Ransom, J. (2018, January 11). *Ten things you should do if your grant proposal is rejected.* Bloomerang. https://bloomerang.co/blog/10-things-you-should-do-if-your-grant-proposal-is-rejected/

Sparks, G. (2018). *Ninety-Four percent of teachers spend their own money on school supplies.* CNN Politics. https://www.cnn.com/2018/05/15/politics/teachers-school-supplies-spending/index.html

Simmons, A. (2019). *Diverse, inclusive and bilingual literacy program.* Innovation Awards: Education First and NoVo Foundation. https://selforteachers.org/innovation-awards

Stombaugh, H. (2014, December 5). *Decision making matrix. Is that grant proposal worth your time?* http://justwrite-solutions.com/decision-making-matrix

Tomlinson, C. (August, 2000). *Differentiation of instruction in the elementary grades.* ERIC digest. ERIC Clearinghouse on Elementary and Early Childhood Education. https://files.eric.ed.gov/fulltext/ED443572.pdf

Wiggins, G., & McTighe, J. (2005). *Understanding by design.* Association for Supervision & Curriculum Development.

Like the Book?

WE ARE SO GLAD THAT YOU ARE HAPPY. SPREAD THE JOY BY:

 Sharing your experience on AMAZON by writing a review.

 Telling your friends and family about it.

 Post about it and tag us.

 FB: bkconsultancy
IG: bk_consultancy

Printed in the USA
CPSIA information can be obtained
at www.ICGtesting.com
LVHW061809190324
774909LV00003B/74

9 781734 852516